ROOM TO THINK 3

Brain Games for
Kids
9 - 12

Copyright © 2022 – Kaye Nutman

All rights reserved. This book or any portion thereof may not be reproduced or used in any manner whatsoever, without the express written permission of the publisher, except for the use of brief quotations in a book review or scholarly journal.

First Printing Mar 2022
oggytheoggdesign
Brighton Victoria Australia

I'd love you to check out this website:
www.kayenutman-writer.com
or Ingram Spark, Amazon, and many other good book shops and sellers, for more books by the author
Kaye Nutman - oggytheoggdesign.

If you'd like a *print at home* version of this book, then you'll find it on my website, and etsy.com too.
https://www.etsy.com/shop/oggytheoggdesign
You are most welcome to join my author group on Facebook at
Kaye Nutman – Author
www.facebook.com/groups/360878484067782

oggytheoggdesign

Dedicated to

All the children I taught in my career, who are now passing on their love of learning to their own young ones.

To my adventurous Great-Nephews and Nieces, who get such enjoyment playing with numbers, writing creatively, and always having fun.

Kaye Nutman - Author

CONTENTS

How to Use this Book	8
Make Your Own Dice	9-10
Make a Sleuth's Headband	11-12
20 Questions	13-19
Colours & Words	20-24
Anagrams	25-37
Ka-Boom	38-46
Labyrinths	47-67
Labyrinths Solutions	68-74
Penalty Points	75-82
Flash Fiction	83-98
Schulte Tables	99-103
Memory Boosters	104-121
Bonus Bookmarks	124-125

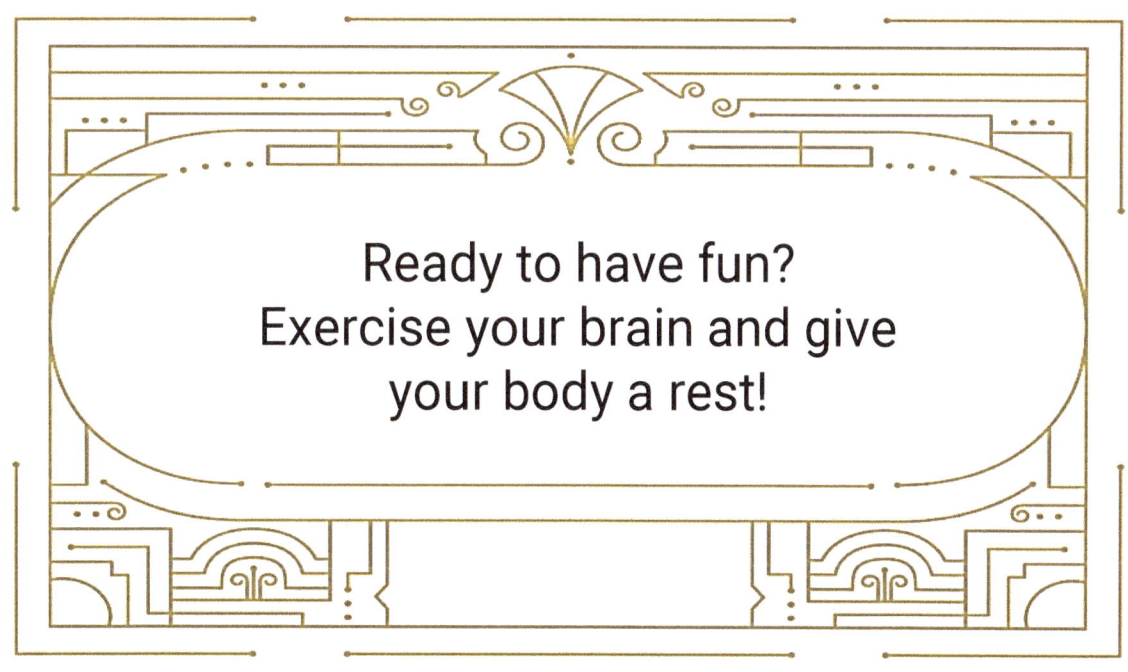

Ready to have fun?
Exercise your brain and give your body a rest!

HOW TO USE THIS BOOK

Welcome to this entertaining book, chock full of addictive games of creativity, strategy and logic – all with the aim of stimulating your growing brain whilst having fun.

❖ You can work your way from beginning to end – in which case you will have achieved a mighty record!
There are 9 categories of game, and 204 individual puzzles or pieces of creativity to have fun with. Varying from 30 seconds to around 30 minutes per game. At the end of each set you can show your emotional response to the games by circling the yellow faces or adding your own emotions.

❖ Or look at the Contents Page and dive into any set that takes your fancy! If it amuses you and you use your brain in a logical, creative or strategic fashion, then you are succeeding. Then flit like a butterfly to the next activity.

❖ Perhaps you'll be directed by a parent or teacher to do certain pages that they think are most appropriate for developing certain skills.

So... explore the power of your brain. Play solo, with a partner, or in a group.

There's ample room to write and room to think!
Feel great as you boost your intelligence and improve concentration, memory and visual motor skills with puzzles, games and other brain building activities.

Interactive and amusing tasks are the perfect way to exercise your brain, improve cognitive skills and make you smarter.

Enjoy!

Need to Make your own dice?

Ways to choose who goes first
- Roll a dice. Highest number goes first.
- Roll 2,3, or 4 dice and add up - *lowest* number goes first.
- Play Rock, Paper, Scissors - one game or best of 3.
- Lowest age goes first, or first birth month of the year.
- Most buttons on your clothes goes first.
- Pick a toy figure. Spin it around. Head points to the winner.
- Choose a shape. Roll the shape dice. The shape on top, wins.

How to use the headband

Cut out all strips. Use a craft knife to cut along both dotted lines on strip A - this is where you will slot a word card in. Stick the end of A to B. Use the lighter grey as a guide; then the end of C to A. Wrap the strip around your head to see where you need to join B to C. Use your fingers to mark where they cross over, then put a pencil mark on the paper which will show you where to stick it together.

C   A   B

Make one each. Laminate, if possible, for strength.

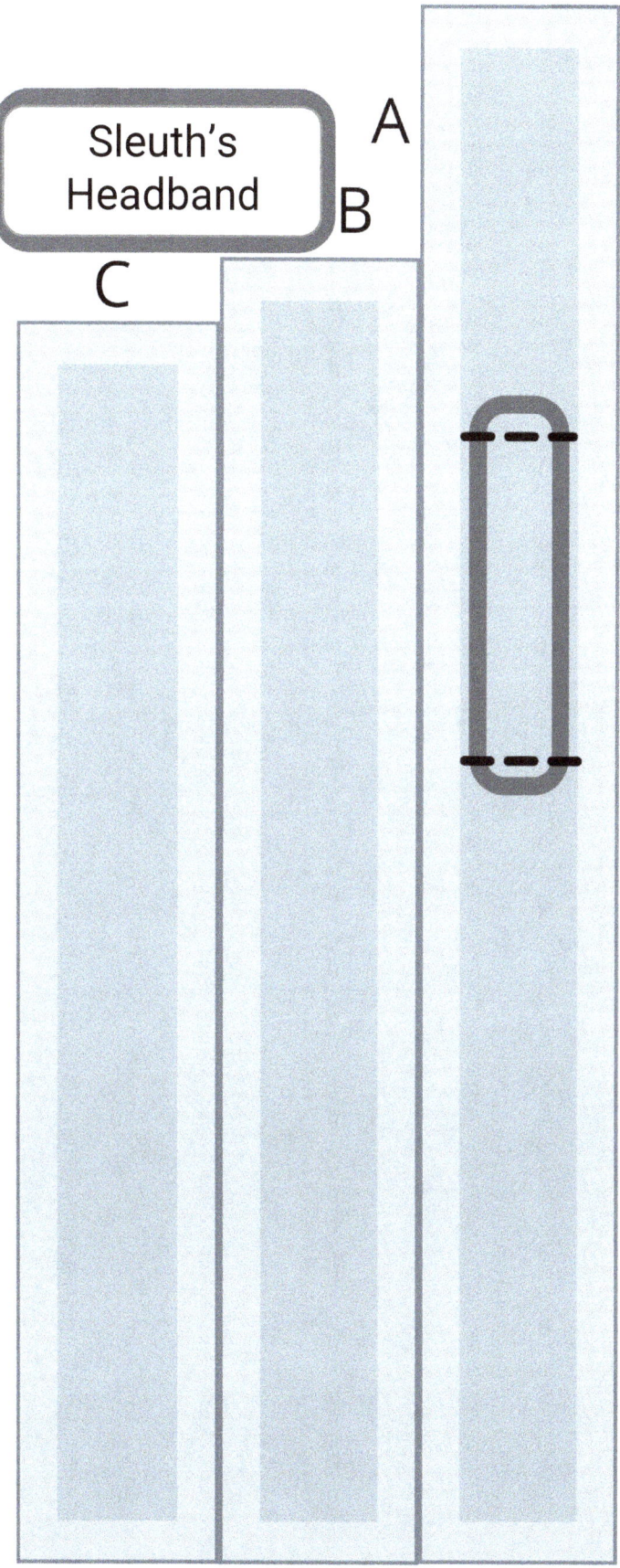

Sleuth's Headband

There's no better way to develop your brain than by having it think up clever questions to ask. But be careful - you only have 20!
Which is why this game is called

20 Questions

This develops Cognitive Thinking.
Cut out your own headband and the name cards from each page, or copy them onto card and make your own. Put one card into the slots without your partner seeing, then pop it on their head!
This reminds you of the word.
Your partner has 20 goes at guessing what the word is. Only YES or NO questions are allowed... such as 'Is it bigger than a horse?"
There are 80 cards, in 5 categories.
After the first 10 questions (keep a tally) you can give a hint if your partner asks for one... such as 'it begins with the letter E'
Have fun!

20 Questions

 **People**

- Queen Elizabeth II
- Walt Disney
- Pablo Picasso
- Angelina Jolie
- Cleopatra
- Tom Hanks
- David Beckham
- Nelson Mandela

- Leonardo da Vinci
- Beethoven
- Darth Vader
- Amelia Earhart
- Harry Potter
- Lady Gaga
- Ed Sheeran
- Greta Thunberg

20 Questions

Places in the World

- Antarctica
- Scotland
- Taj Mahal, India
- Hollywood
- New Zealand
- Uluru Rock, Australia
- Statue of Liberty
- Big Ben, London

- Great Barrier Reef
- Machu Picchu, Peru
- Pyramids, Egypt
- Rome, Italy
- Great Wall of China
- Eiffel Tower, Paris
- Lego Land
- Mount Fuji, Japan

20 Questions

 **Famous Objects**

- Mask of Tutankamun
- Easter Island Heads
- Tyrannosaurus Rex Skeleton
- Space Shuttle
- Nazca Desert Drawings
- Seated Buddha
- Inca Gold Llama
- Shadow Puppets

- Stonehenge
- Terracotta Warriors
- Ned Kelly's Armour
- The Crown Jewels
- The Rosetta Stone
- Lewis Chessmen
- Double Headed Serpent
- Throne of Weapons

20 Questions

Jobs beginning with P

- Plumber
- Personal Trainer
- Painter
- Porter
- Pathologist
- Package Designer
- Photographer
- Pediatrician
- Paramedic
- Police Officer
- President
- Pharmacist
- Personal Banker
- Packer
- Pastry Chef
- Pilot

20 Questions

World Capitals

- Tokyo - Japan
- Paris - France
- Berlin - Germany
- Cairo - Egypt
- Beijing - China
- Delhi - India
- Athens - Greece
- Washington DC - USA

- London - England
- Moscow - Russia
- Madrid - Spain
- Rome - Italy
- Bangkok - Thailand
- Canberra - Australia
- Wellington - New Zealand
- Vienna - Austria

HOW DID YOU FEEL ABOUT THE GAMES YOU PLAYED?
CIRCLE ANY THAT APPLY.
YOU CAN EVEN ADD YOUR OWN!

Colours and Words

This game can mess with your brain!
Look at the words below. You are asked to call the colour of the word (<u>not</u> to read out the name). So blue would be called out as red. You can play this alone, or with another player who keeps a close eye on whether you are correct. Your task is just to look at the <u>colours</u> while ignoring the typed words.
So... **say the colour not the word**.

Player 1 Score ⬅┈┈┈➡ 6

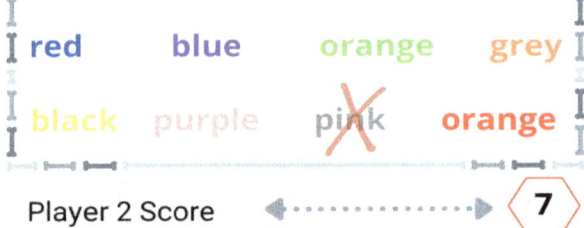

Player 2 Score ⬅┈┈┈➡ 7

Colours used in this game

Quick Practice

- Blue
- Black
- Grey
- Green
- Purple
- Pink
- Red
- Orange
- Yellow

COLOURS & WORDS

orange   green   pink   yellow

purple   grey   red   black

Player 2 Score

orange   blue   pink   purple

black   red   green   yellow

Player 1 Score

pink   purple   orange   blue

black   green   grey   yellow

Player 2 Score

COLOURS & WORDS

pink   grey   blue   purple

black   pink   red   yellow

Player 2 Score

blue   purple   pink   yellow

grey   orange   green   black

Player 1 Score

orange   red   black   grey

yellow   blue   grey   red

Player 2 Score

COLOURS & WORDS

red   blue   green   black

pink   orange   pink   grey

Player 2 Score

red   orange   grey   yellow

blue   black   green   pink

Player 1 Score

orange   blue   pink   red

grey   black   yellow   purple

Player 2 Score

COLOURS & WORDS

black   grey   purple   green

yellow   purple   green   black

Player 1 Score

orange   blue   pink   purple

black   red   yellow   green

Player 2 Score

pink   purple   orange   blue

black   green   grey   yellow

Player 1 Score

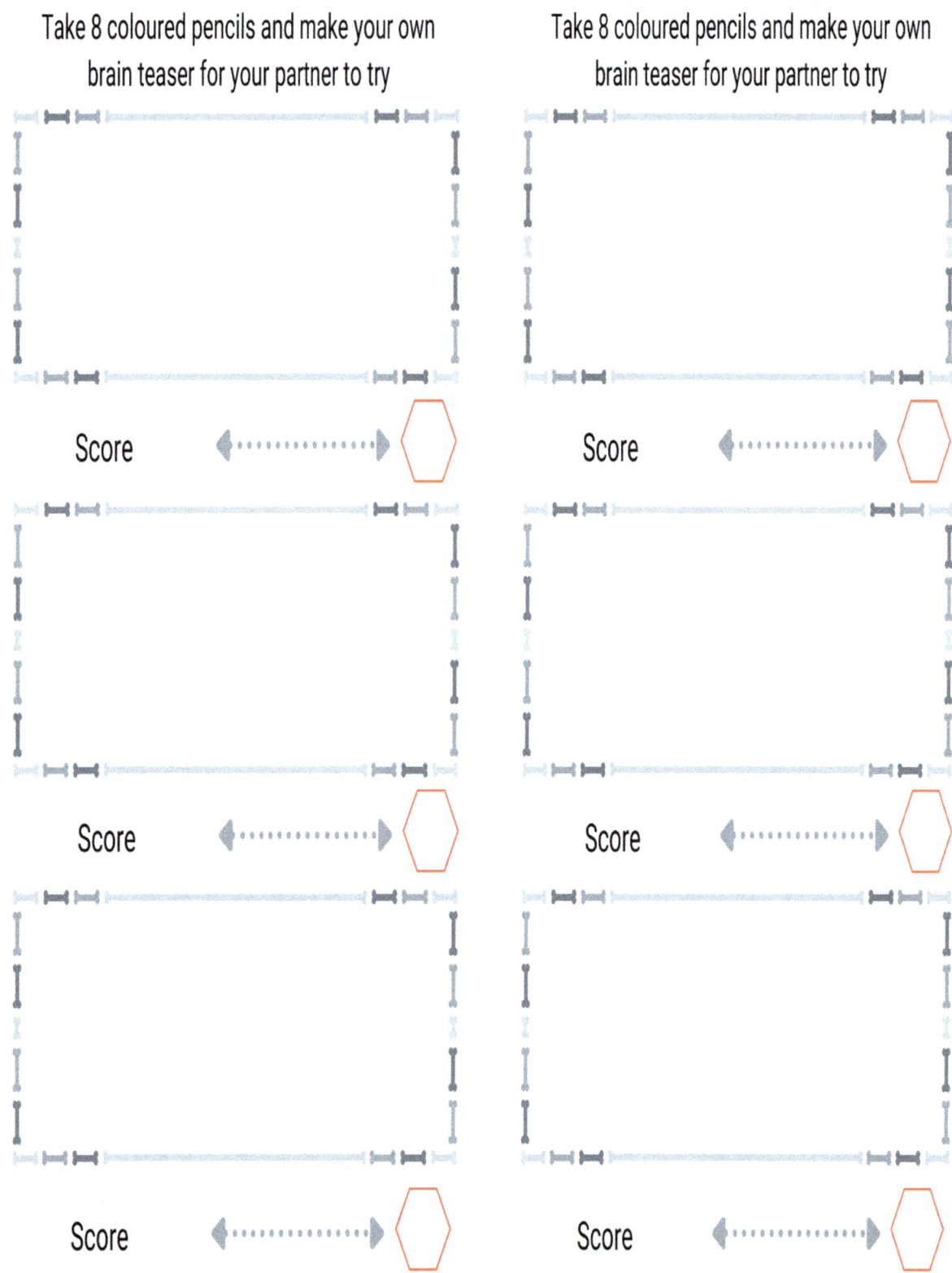

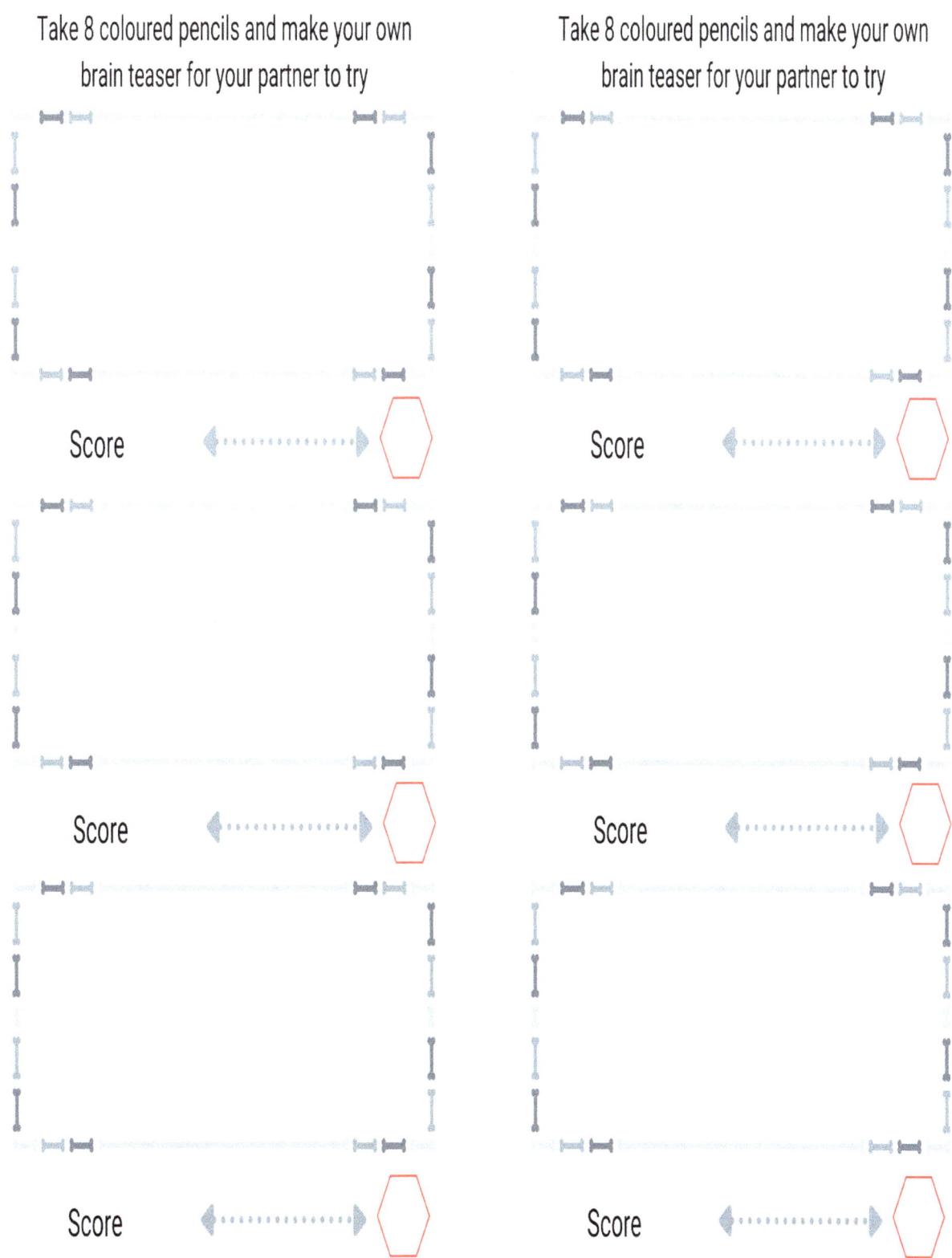

HOW DID YOU FEEL ABOUT THE GAMES YOU PLAYED?
CIRCLE ANY THAT APPLY.
YOU CAN EVEN ADD YOUR OWN!

Anagrams

What to do

Make as many words or phrases as you can from the titles on each page.

You can use the boxes to work out how many of each letter there are, to help avoid errors, or jump straight in.

If you write in the boxes do this before using a 2 minute timer. Then GO!

Ask someone to check your answers. Add up the number of words or phrases - giving 1 point for each correct word and 2 points for each phrase.

A Day in the Garden

A	D	Y	I	N	T	H
3	2	1	1	2	1	1

E	G	R	
2	1	1	

head
heard

Nine grand
Dry Den
dread   dehydrate
I Need an Ant
Grey Diner
thin grade
near an idea
tread   angered   great

Number of Words	Number of Phrases
7	6

19

Entangled Buildings

Number of Words	Number of Phrases

Inside the Cathedral

Number of Words	Number of Phrases

Pecan Power Nuts

Number of Words	Number of Phrases

Fiery Firmament

| Number of Words | Number of Phrases |

Reptile Skin

Number of Words	Number of Phrases

Red Sky at Night

| Number of Words | Number of Phrases |

Any Citrus Fruits

| Number of Words | Number of Phrases |

A Pebbled Beach

Number of Words	Number of Phrases

Rain on the Windowpane

Number of Words	Number of Phrases

Where's my Shoe?

Number of Words	Number of Phrases

HOW DID YOU FEEL ABOUT THE GAMES YOU PLAYED?
CIRCLE ANY THAT APPLY.
YOU CAN EVEN ADD YOUR OWN!

How to Play
Ka-Boom!

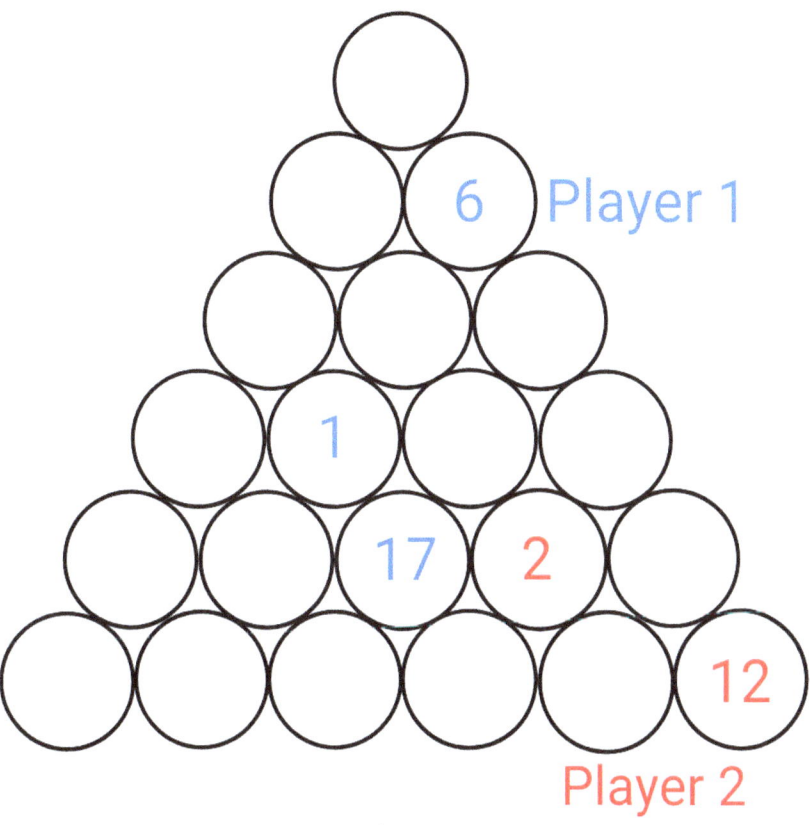

For Two Players

A Game of stratetgy. Each player chooses a different colour pen.
Take turns - fill the pile with ten numbers between 1 and 20;
there is one blank circle left - the Bomb!
Any numbers that surround the bomb are within
the blast zone and are eliminated (Ka-boom!).
Each player adds up the numbers they have left.
The winner is the one with the highest score.

Ka-Boom!

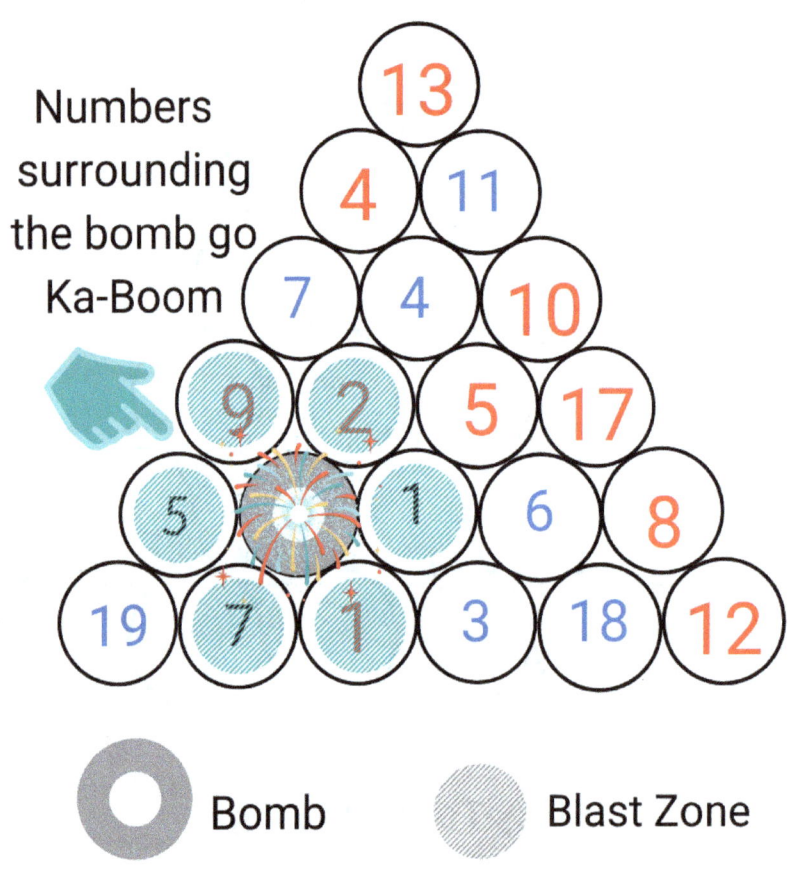

Numbers surrounding the bomb go Ka-Boom

○ Bomb   ▨ Blast Zone

Blue Pen - 19+3+18+6+4+7+11=68
Red pen - 12+8+17+5+10+4+13=69

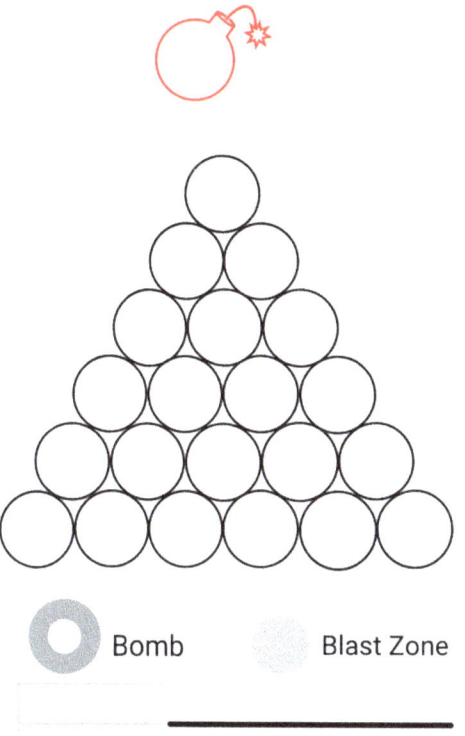
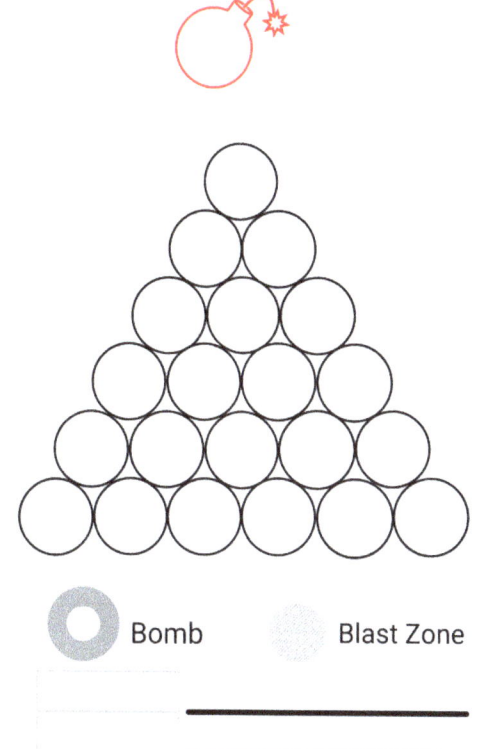
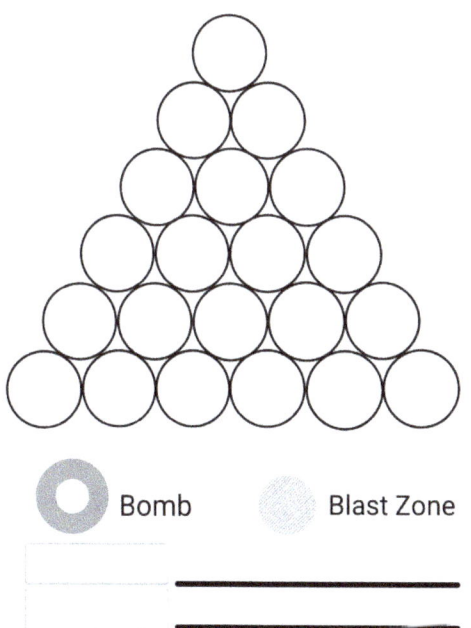
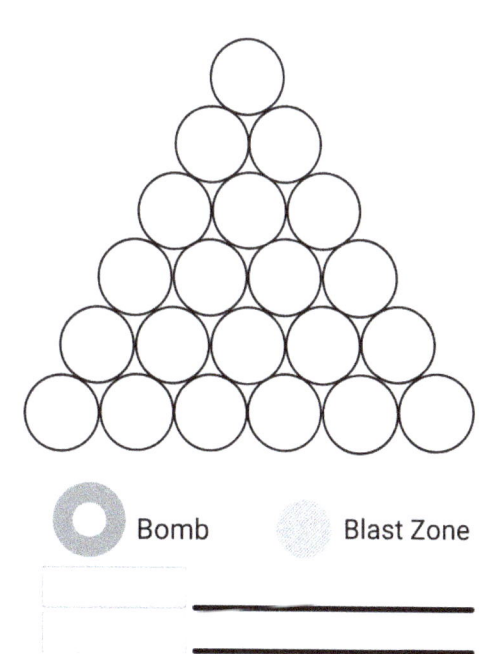

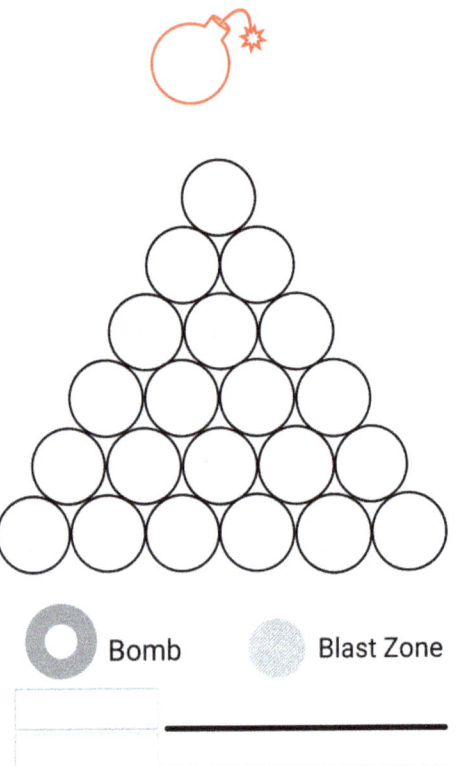

● Bomb   ● Blast Zone

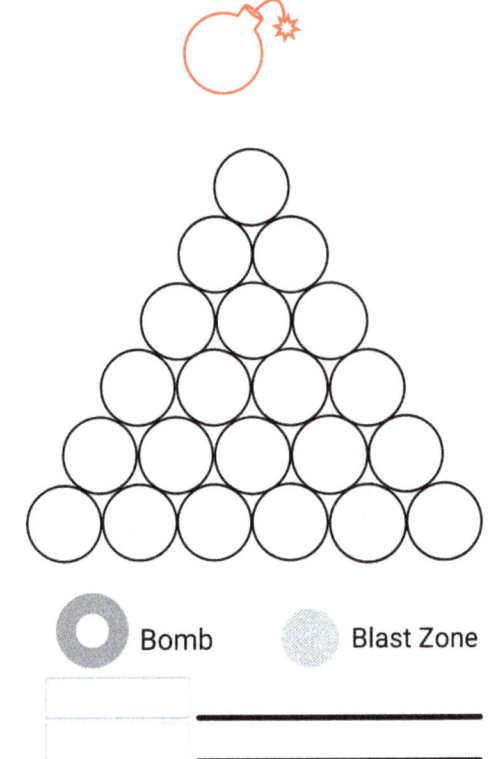

● Bomb   ● Blast Zone

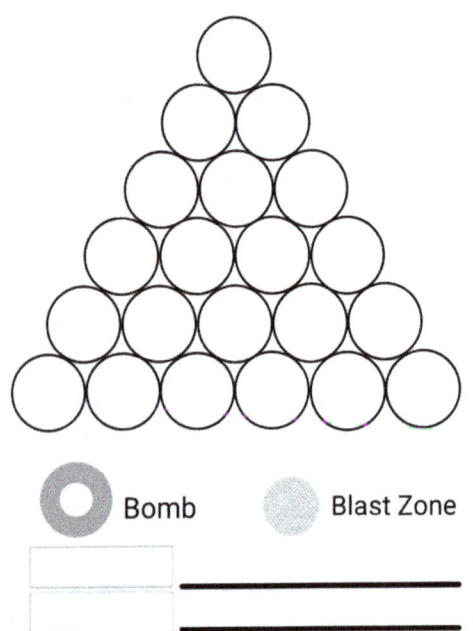

● Bomb   ● Blast Zone

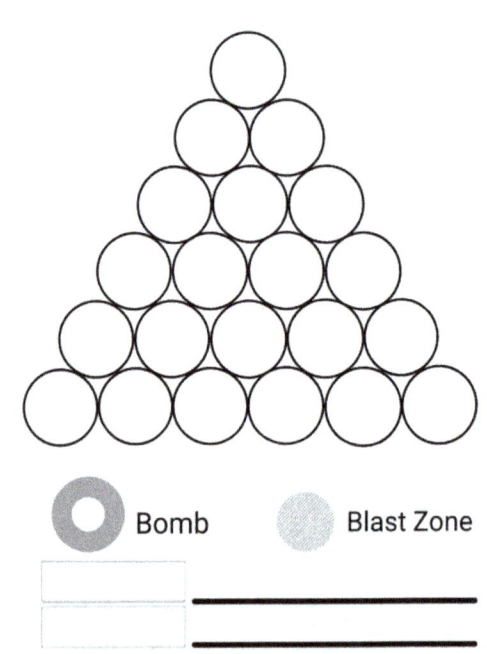

● Bomb   ● Blast Zone

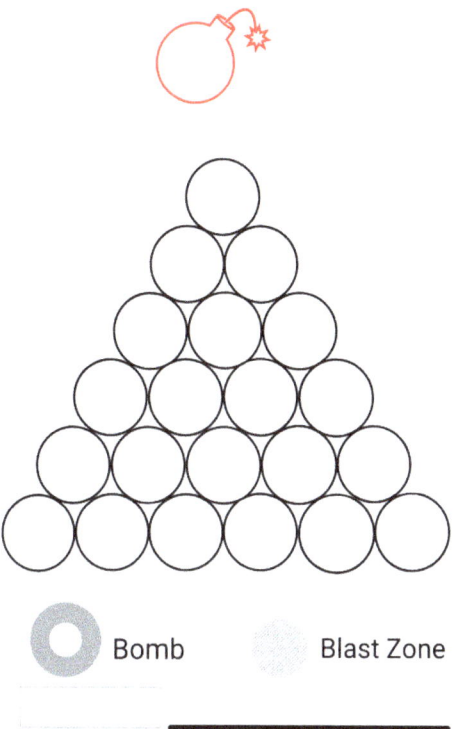
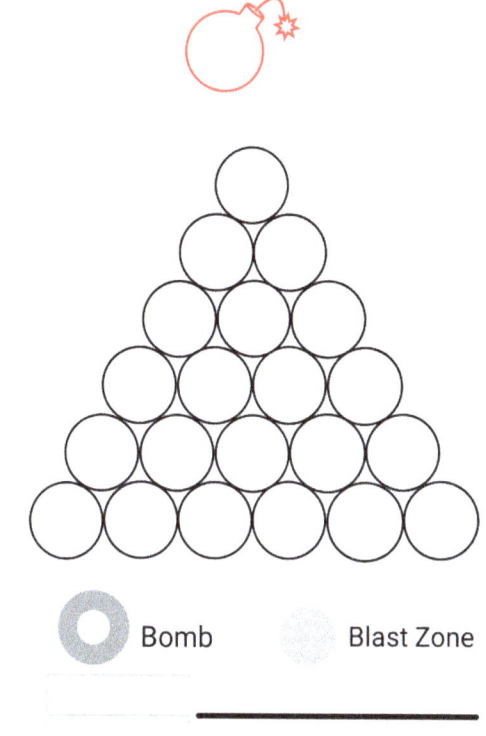
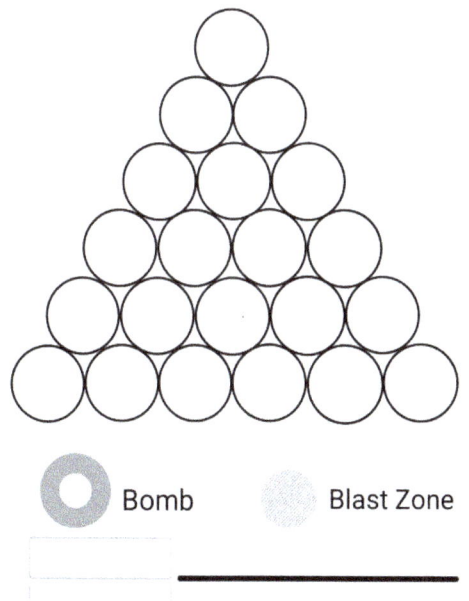
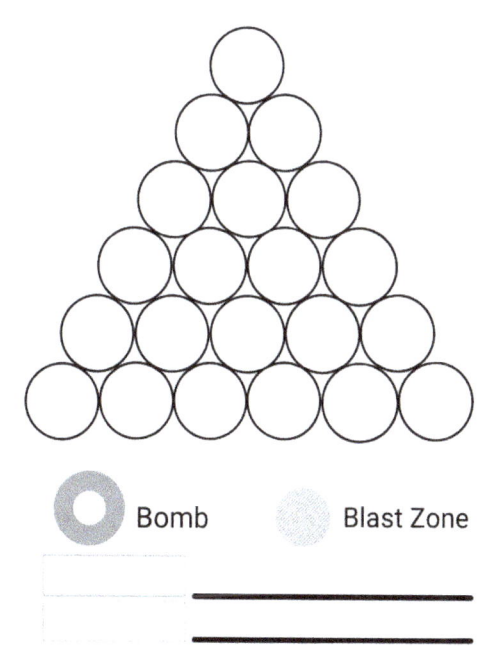

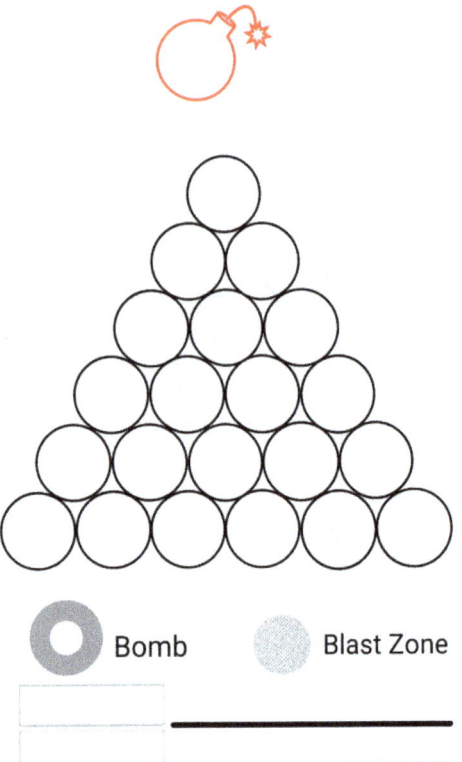

○ Bomb ● Blast Zone

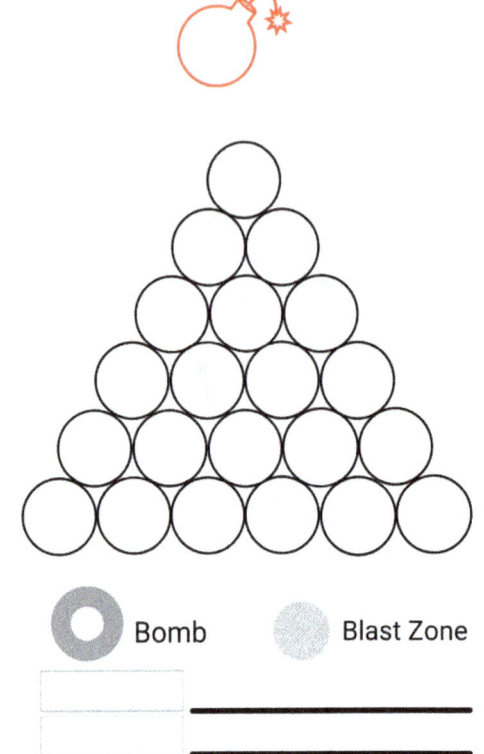

○ Bomb ● Blast Zone

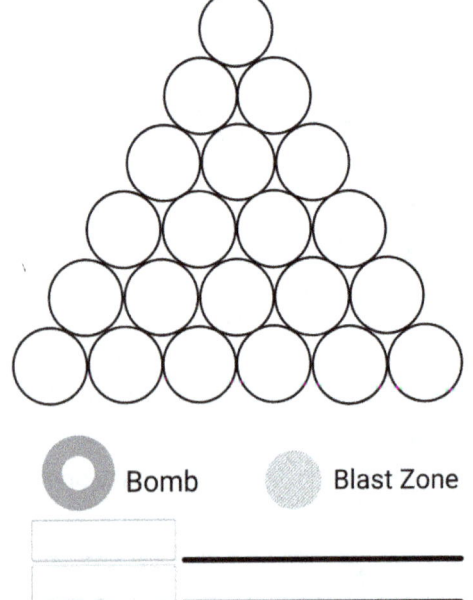

○ Bomb ● Blast Zone

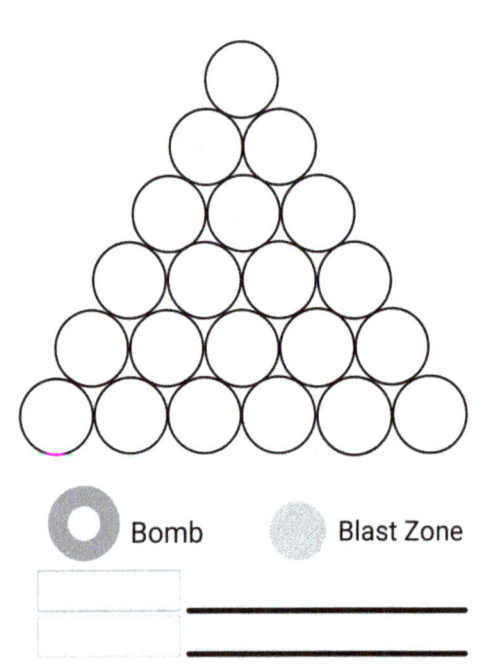

○ Bomb ● Blast Zone

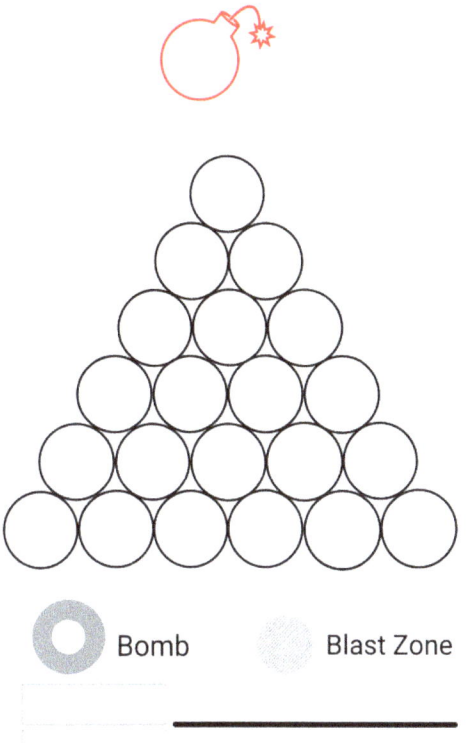

○ Bomb ● Blast Zone

_____
_____

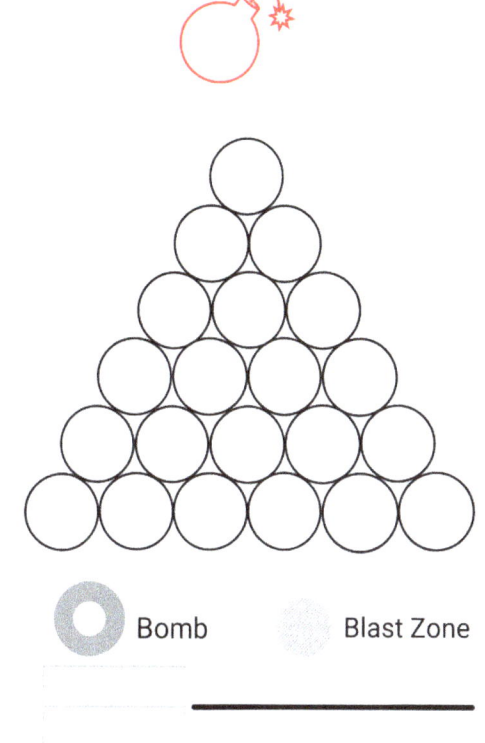

○ Bomb ● Blast Zone

_____
_____

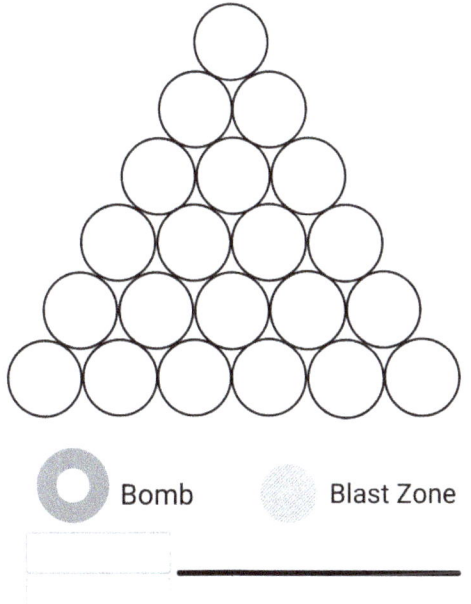

○ Bomb ● Blast Zone

_____
_____

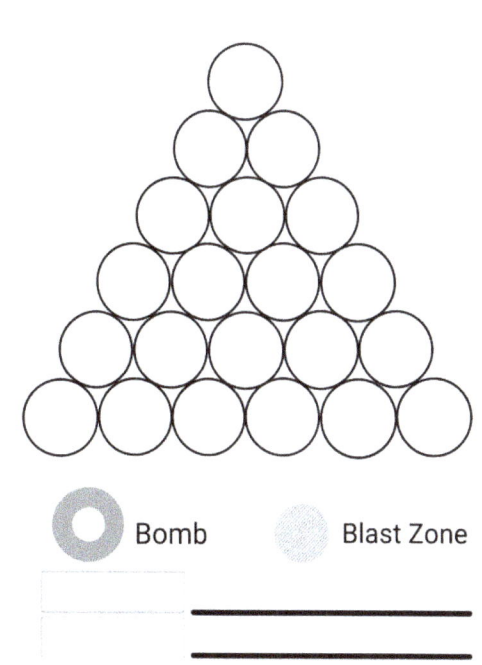

○ Bomb ● Blast Zone

_____
_____

HOW DID YOU FEEL ABOUT THE GAMES YOU PLAYED?
CIRCLE ANY THAT APPLY.
YOU CAN EVEN ADD YOUR OWN!

GROUP GAME   GAME FOR 2

IT WAS SO FUNNY   I LIKE QUIET WORK   IT WAS OKAY

I LOVED IT   MEH...

THIS WAS FUN   IT WAS CONFUSING

AHEM... NAILED IT!   NEW TO ME

Labyrinths
(Mazes)

"A confusing set of connecting passages or paths in which it is easy to get lost."

> You will need a pencil and a clean eraser. It is pleasing to get the pathway correct first time, but some of these labyrinths are tricky! Once you have it worked out you can go over the route with a coloured pencil if you wish.

Labyrinths

Squirrel Cyril stored his acorns for winter, but has forgotten where they are. Help him find the way.

Labyrinths

Bonnie Fox needs to find her way to her den. Which trail should she take?

Labyrinths

Brodie bee is seeking a way to meet up with his friends in the meadow.

Labyrinths

Joseph needs to get his gem stones to the crushing plant at the top. Help him push the cart from deep in the centre of the mine to the entrance.

Labyrinths

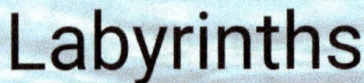

Mama Duck needs to get to her ducklings in the reeds. Help her get there.

Labyrinths

Jenson is taking his car to the garage, but can't remember the way. Which route should he take?

Labyrinths

Which way does the water need to flow to fill the bowl at the bottom?

Labyrinths

Harry, the cheeky monkey is very hungry. He remembers hiding some bananas in the maze, but... which path should he take?

Labyrinths

Only one of the children can get to the play house in the jungle. Which one is it?

Labyrinths

Edith the Eagle has spotted her prey in the centre of the maze. Which route will she take?

Labyrinths

The amazing knight on his white steed is hurrying to rescue the princess from the dragon. Can you get him there quickly?

Labyrinths

The rocket is on its way to the fireworks display. Help it reach its target.

Labyrinths

Which cat gets to sit on Jessie's lap?

Labyrinths

Help the children playing superheroes to escape the mad scientist. Can you get them to the safety of the red door?

Labyrinths

Tillie the Tiger fell asleep. Her cubs sneaked though the labyrinth but couldn't find their way back.
Help Tillie get to them.

Labyrinths

Six ants in a line need to get through to their queen. Which way should they go?

Labyrinths

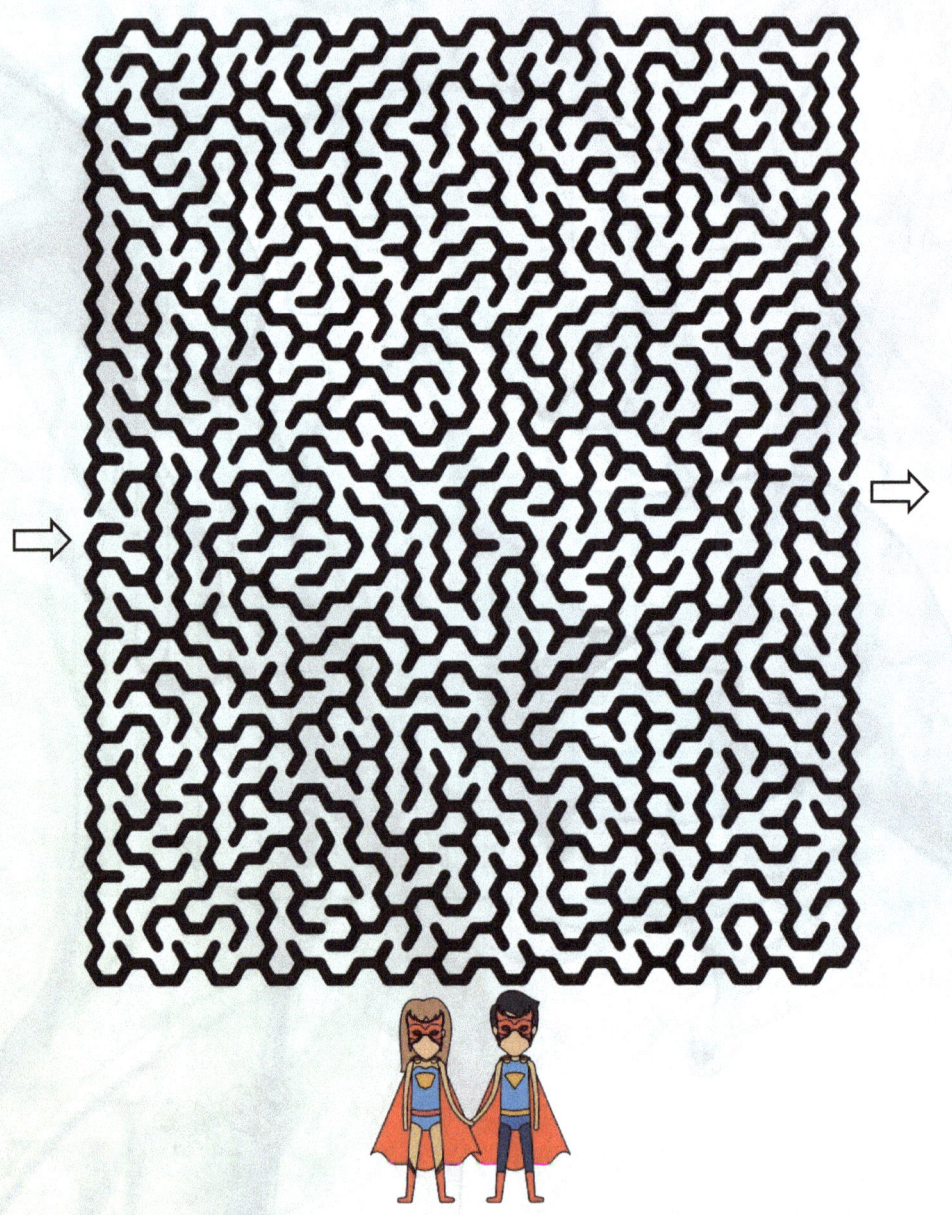

These trainee superheroes have to
find their way through the maze.
They are asking for your help.
Go for it!

Labyrinths

This twinkling star is looking for her friends. Get her safely through the maze to join them.

Labyrinths

The palomino pony can smell the fresh green grass in the meadow. Help her get there.

Labyrinths

These families are on their way to the play park. Help them take a pleasant walk on the way.

Labyrinths Solutions

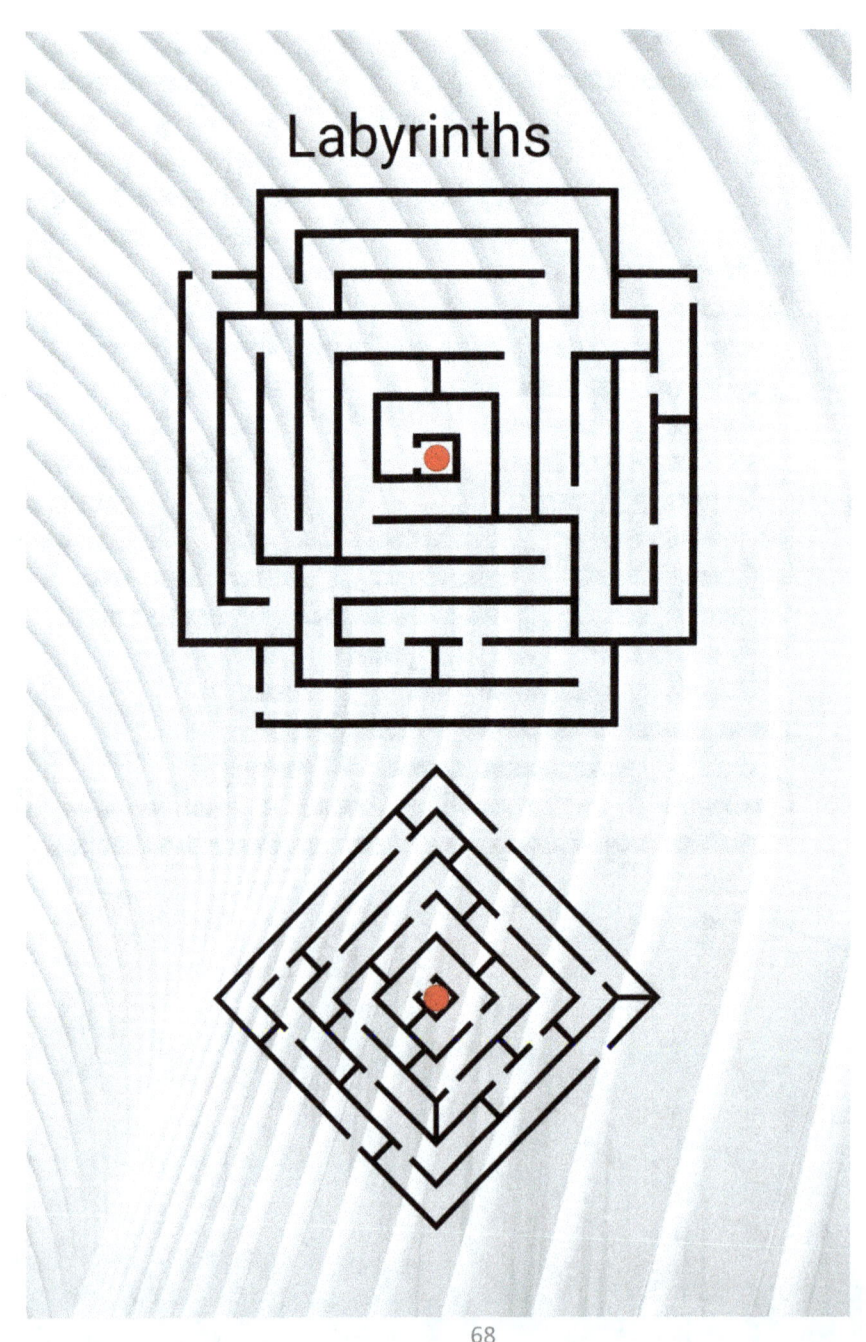

Labyrinths

Labyrinths

Labyrinths

Labyrinths

Labyrinths

Labyrinths

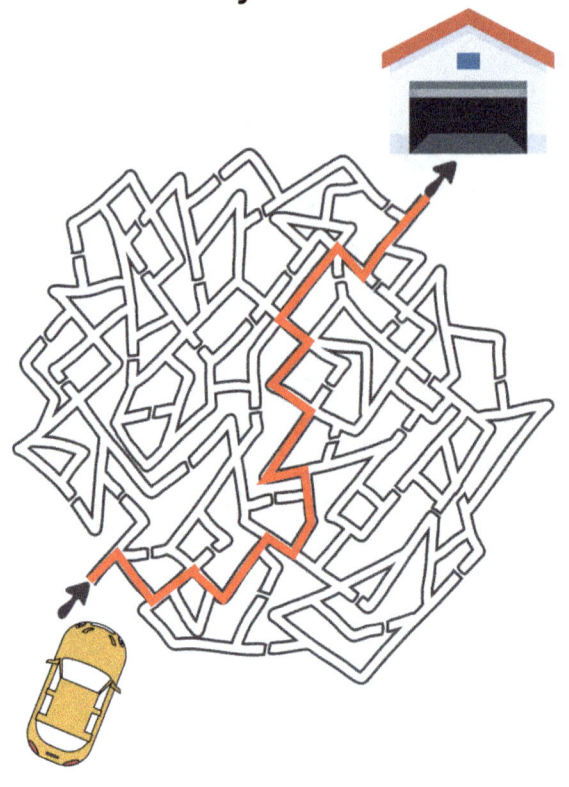

Labyrinths

Labyrinths

Labyrinths

Labyrinths

Labyrinths

Labyrinths

Labyrinths

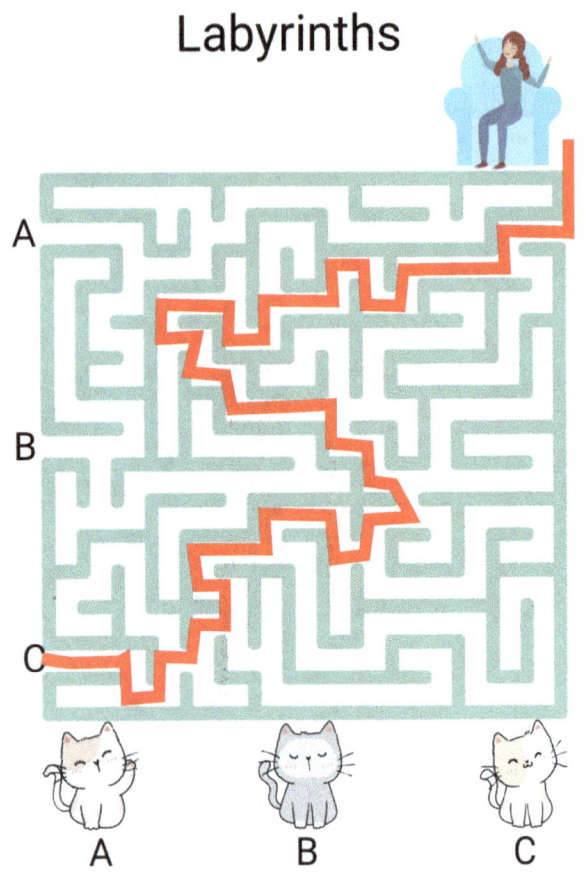

Labyrinths

Labyrinths

Labyrinths

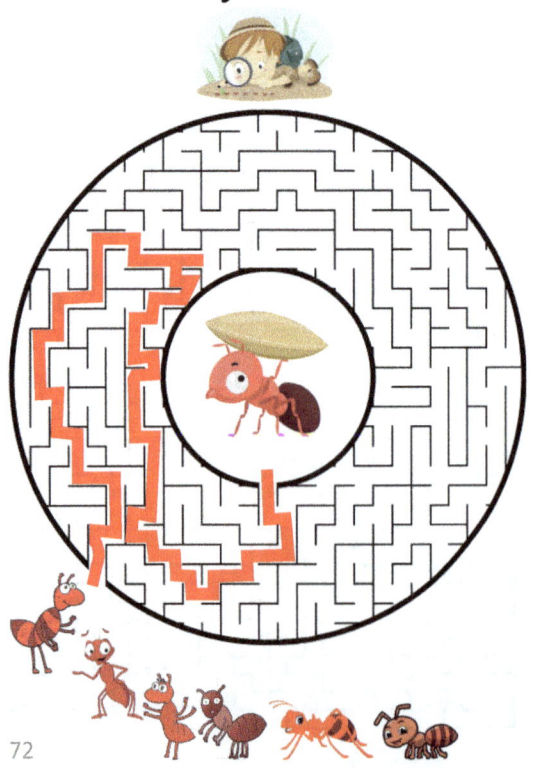

Labyrinths

Labyrinths

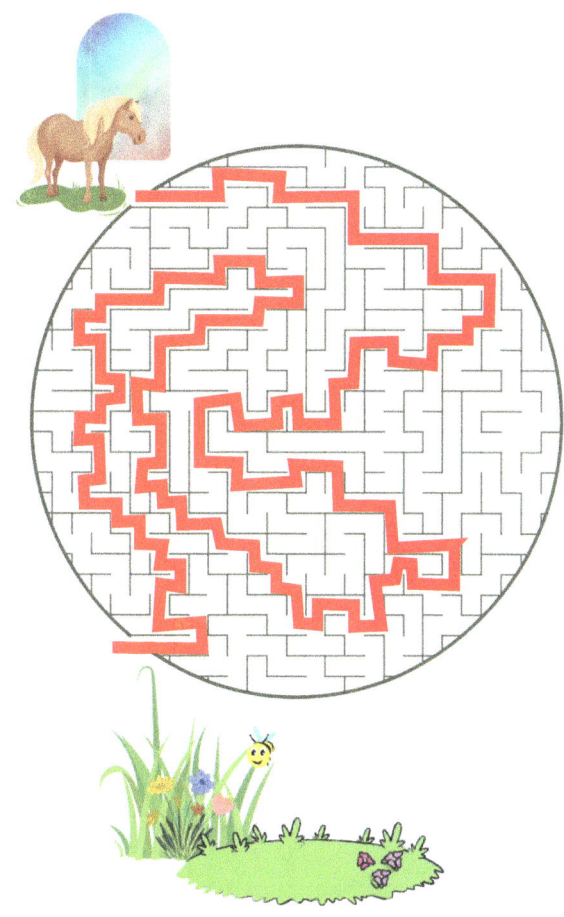

Labyrinths

Labyrinths

HOW DID YOU FEEL ABOUT THE GAMES YOU PLAYED?
CIRCLE ANY THAT APPLY.
YOU CAN EVEN ADD YOUR OWN!

GROUP GAME   GAME FOR 2

IT WAS SO FUNNY   I LIKE QUIET WORK   IT WAS OKAY

I LOVED IT   MEH...

THIS WAS FUN   IT WAS CONFUSING

AHEM... NAILED IT!   NEW TO ME

Penalty Points

A game for 2 Players.

Player **1** thinks of a number between 1 and 10, and secretly writes it in the box (use a hand or piece of paper to keep it hidden from Player 2).

Player **2** guesses what the number is, and writes their guess **with a circle round it** in the box on their side.

When Player 1 reveals their number they then see if there is a difference between the two numbers. Take away one number from the other and write that number in Player 2 Penalty Box.

Then reverse roles, with Player 1 guessing.

After 6 games, add up the total of all Penalty Points. The person with the **lowest total** wins!

You can adjust the difficulty of the game from numbers between 1 and 10 to numbers between 1 -20, or 1 - 100.

PENALTY POINTS

Player 1	1 Penalty Box	2 Penalty Box	Player 2
Total Penalty Points			Total Penalty Points

PENALTY POINTS

Player 1	1 Penalty Box	2 Penalty Box	Player 2
Total Penalty Points			Total Penalty Points

PENALTY POINTS

Player 1	1 Penalty Box	2 Penalty Box	Player 2
Total Penalty Points			Total Penalty Points

PENALTY POINTS

Player 1	1 Penalty Box	2 Penalty Box	Player 2
Total Penalty Points			Total Penalty Points

PENALTY POINTS

Player 1	1 Penalty Box	2 Penalty Box	Player 2
Total Penalty Points			Total Penalty Points

PENALTY POINTS

Player 1	1 Penalty Box	2 Penalty Box	Player 2
Total Penalty Points			Total Penalty Points

PENALTY POINTS

Player 1	1 Penalty Box	2 Penalty Box	Player 2
Total Penalty Points			Total Penalty Points

PENALTY POINTS

Player 1	1 Penalty Box	2 Penalty Box	Player 2
Total Penalty Points			Total Penalty Points

PENALTY POINTS

Player 1	1 Penalty Box	2 Penalty Box	Player 2
Total Penalty Points			Total Penalty Points

PENALTY POINTS

Player 1	1 Penalty Box	2 Penalty Box	Player 2
Total Penalty Points			Total Penalty Points

PENALTY POINTS

Player 1	1 Penalty Box	2 Penalty Box	Player 2
Total Penalty Points			Total Penalty Points

PENALTY POINTS

Player 1	1 Penalty Box	2 Penalty Box	Player 2
Total Penalty Points			Total Penalty Points

PENALTY POINTS

Player 1	1 Penalty Box	2 Penalty Box	Player 2
Total Penalty Points			Total Penalty Points

PENALTY POINTS

Player 1	1 Penalty Box	2 Penalty Box	Player 2
Total Penalty Points			Total Penalty Points

PENALTY POINTS

Player 1	1 Penalty Box	2 Penalty Box	Player 2
Total Penalty Points			Total Penalty Points

PENALTY POINTS

Player 1	1 Penalty Box	2 Penalty Box	Player 2
Total Penalty Points			Total Penalty Points

HOW DID YOU FEEL ABOUT THE GAMES YOU PLAYED?
CIRCLE ANY THAT APPLY.
YOU CAN EVEN ADD YOUR OWN!

GROUP GAME   GAME FOR 2

IT WAS SO FUNNY   I LIKE QUIET WORK   IT WAS OKAY

I LOVED IT   MEH...

THIS WAS FUN   IT WAS CONFUSING

AHEM... NAILED IT!   NEW TO ME

Flash Fiction

Very Short Stories
IMAGERY

What we hear
Music
Silence
Traffic

Shape
Colour
Patterns
What we see

Taste
Sweet
Sour
Salty

Touch
Temperature
Movement
e.g. the wind
Texture

Fragrance
e.g. perfume
Odour
e.g. rotten vegetables
Smell

Emotion – what do you want your reader to feel - sad, happy, angry...
Character – who is this story about?
Imagery – what strong imagery will your story use? Touch, Taste, Sight, Hearing, Seeing.
Inciting incident – where will you start your story? Maybe show something strange your character is doing to spark interest.
Hook ending – what will your twist be?

―――・✦・―――

Which has better imagery?
"He kicked the ball savagely and the musician cried out in pain"
or "He kicked the ball. It hit the musician."

Create Flash Fiction

- dancers
- angry
- disco
- red shoes
- smell
- stranger

Write a short story using the six words above.
You can continue on the next page.

Create Flash Fiction

- dancers
- angry
- disco
- red shoes
- smell
- stranger

Create Flash Fiction

- motor bike
- snob
- girl
- high-rise appartment
- old man
- funny

Write a short story using the six words above.
You can continue on the next page.

Create Flash Fiction

- motor bike
- snob
- girl
- high-rise appartment
- old man
- funny

Create Flash Fiction

- shoes
- ungrateful
- secretary
- race
- judge
- laughter

Write a short story using the six words above.
You can continue on the next page.

Create Flash Fiction

- shoes
- ungrateful
- secretary
- race
- judge
- laughter

Create Flash Fiction

| great-aunt | dream | planet |
| wind | astronaut | stones |

Write a short story using the six words above.
You can continue on the next page.

Create Flash Fiction

- sailor
- kind
- beach
- notebook
- party
- musician

Write a short story using the six words above.
You can continue on the next page.

Create Flash Fiction

- sailor
- kind
- beach
- notebook
- party
- musician

Create a Story

- different
- children
- daily
- holidays
- delighted
- captain

Write a short story using the six words above.
You can continue on the next page.

Create a Story

- different
- children
- daily
- holidays
- delighted
- captain

Create a Story

- generous
- party
- delighted
- city
- spy
- outcast

Write a short story using the six words above.
You can continue on the next page.

Create a Story

- generous
- party
- delighted
- city
- spy
- outcast

HOW DID YOU FEEL ABOUT THE GAMES YOU PLAYED?
CIRCLE ANY THAT APPLY.
YOU CAN EVEN ADD YOUR OWN!

GROUP GAME

GAME FOR 2

IT WAS SO FUNNY

I LIKE QUIET WORK

IT WAS OKAY

I LOVED IT

MEH...

THIS WAS FUN

IT WAS CONFUSING

AHEM... NAILED IT!

NEW TO ME

Schulte Tables

10	4	18	7	12
24	14	22	3	9
1	23	15	21	19
20	5	2	11	16
13	8	25	17	6

RULES

Start a timer for 30 seconds.
Find the numbers 1 - 25, in the correct order.
Stop the clock!
Write down the time it took you.

seconds

You can use a pencil or your finger.

SCHULTE TABLES

10	4	18	7	12
24	14	22	3	9
1	23	15	21	19
20	5	2	11	16
13	8	25	17	6

RULES

Start a timer for 30 seconds.
Find the numbers 1 - 25, in the correct order.
Stop the clock!
Write down the time it took you.

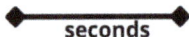 seconds

You can use a pencil or your finger.

SCHULTE TABLES

19	3	4	6	8
18	15	13	9	20
1	10	24	22	11
12	14	2	21	7
16	23	25	17	5

RULES

Start a timer for 30 seconds.
Find the numbers 1 - 25, in the correct order.
Stop the clock!
Write down the time it took you.

━━━━ seconds

You can use a pencil or your finger.

SCHULTE TABLES

11	7	5	24	21
14	15	23	17	20
22	10	6	1	19
18	12	25	8	16
3	13	2	9	4

RULES

Start a timer for 30 seconds.
Find the numbers 1 - 25, in the correct order.
Stop the clock!
Write down the time it took you.

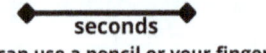 seconds

You can use a pencil or your finger.

MAKE YOUR OWN SCHULTE TABLE

Write the numbers 1 - 25 in the boxes
in random order. Give it to a partner.
Start a timer for 30 seconds.
They find the numbers 1 - 25, in the correct order.
Stop the clock!
Write down the time it took you.

MAKE YOUR OWN SCHULTE TABLE

Write the numbers 1 - 25 in the boxes
in random order. Give it to a partner.
Start a timer for 30 seconds.
They find the numbers 1 - 25, in the correct order.
Stop the clock!
Write down the time it took you.

MAKE YOUR OWN SCHULTE TABLE

Write the numbers 1 - 25 in the boxes
in random order. Give it to a partner.
Start a timer for 30 seconds.
They find the numbers 1 - 25, in the correct order.
Stop the clock!
Write down the time it took you.

MAKE YOUR OWN SCHULTE TABLE

Write the numbers 1 - 25 in the boxes
in random order. Give it to a partner.
Start a timer for 30 seconds.
They find the numbers 1 - 25, in the correct order.
Stop the clock!
Write down the time it took you.

MAKE YOUR OWN SCHULTE TABLE

Write the numbers 1 - 25 in the boxes
in random order. Give it to a partner.
Start a timer for 30 seconds.
They find the numbers 1 - 25, in the correct order.
Stop the clock!
Write down the time it took you.

MAKE YOUR OWN SCHULTE TABLE

Write the numbers 1 - 25 in the boxes
in random order. Give it to a partner.
Start a timer for 30 seconds.
They find the numbers 1 - 25, in the correct order.
Stop the clock!
Write down the time it took you.

MAKE YOUR OWN SCHULTE TABLE

Write the numbers 1 - 25 in the boxes
in random order. Give it to a partner.
Start a timer for 30 seconds.
They find the numbers 1 - 25, in the correct order.
Stop the clock!
Write down the time it took you.

MAKE YOUR OWN SCHULTE TABLE

Write the numbers 1 - 25 in the boxes
in random order. Give it to a partner.
Start a timer for 30 seconds.
They find the numbers 1 - 25, in the correct order.
Stop the clock!
Write down the time it took you.

MAKE YOUR OWN SCHULTE TABLE

Write the numbers 1 - 25 in the boxes
in random order. Give it to a partner.
Start a timer for 30 seconds.
They find the numbers 1 - 25, in the correct order.
Stop the clock!
Write down the time it took you.

HOW DID YOU FEEL ABOUT THE GAMES YOU PLAYED?
CIRCLE ANY THAT APPLY.
YOU CAN EVEN ADD YOUR OWN!

Memory Boosters

Chunking (Grouping)

Chunking helps improve recall in memory games... the sillier the better!
Visualise this...

A Koala clutching a toy yacht - on the back of a truck - whilst balancing a jug on his head.

Yoyo boy with a green watch on his wrist - a rose in his teeth - under a rainbow umbrella.

Maybe imagine you are the Koala or the boy.

jelly   sunshine
   xylophone
whale   weekend
   skates
kangaroo   salad

Chunking (Grouping)

Chunking helps improve recall in memory games... the sillier the better!
Visualise this...

A kangaroo on skates - playing the xylophone - in the sunshine

Jelly wobbling on a plate next to salad - at a weekend party attended by a whale

Maybe imagine you are the kangaroo or at the party.

Memory Booster

Study the words or images for **60 seconds**, then list as many as you can remember on the next page.

My Mood Today. Circle one.

Happy

Calm   Content

Hopeful   Confident

Unhappy   Anxious

Insecure   Fearful

Other

_____

Opposite hand exercise!
Doodle one of the words or pictures above with your non-dominant hand.

Sleep Quality Last Night:

Super!   Good   Restless   Poor

Memory Booster

List as many words as you can remember from the previous page... no peeking!

New Word for YOU

vexillology

the study of flags

Use it in a sentence:

_____

_____

_____

Memory Booster

Study the words or images for **60 seconds**, then list as many as you can remember on the next page.

tree   flower
stem   girl
corn   apple
cherry   nut

My Mood Today.
Circle one.

Happy

Calm Content

Hopeful Confident

Unhappy Anxious

Insecure Fearful

Other

_____

Opposite hand exercise!
Doodle one of the words or pictures above with your non-dominant hand.

Sleep Quality Last Night:

Super!   Good   Restless   Poor

Memory Booster

List as many words as you can remember from the previous page... no peeking!

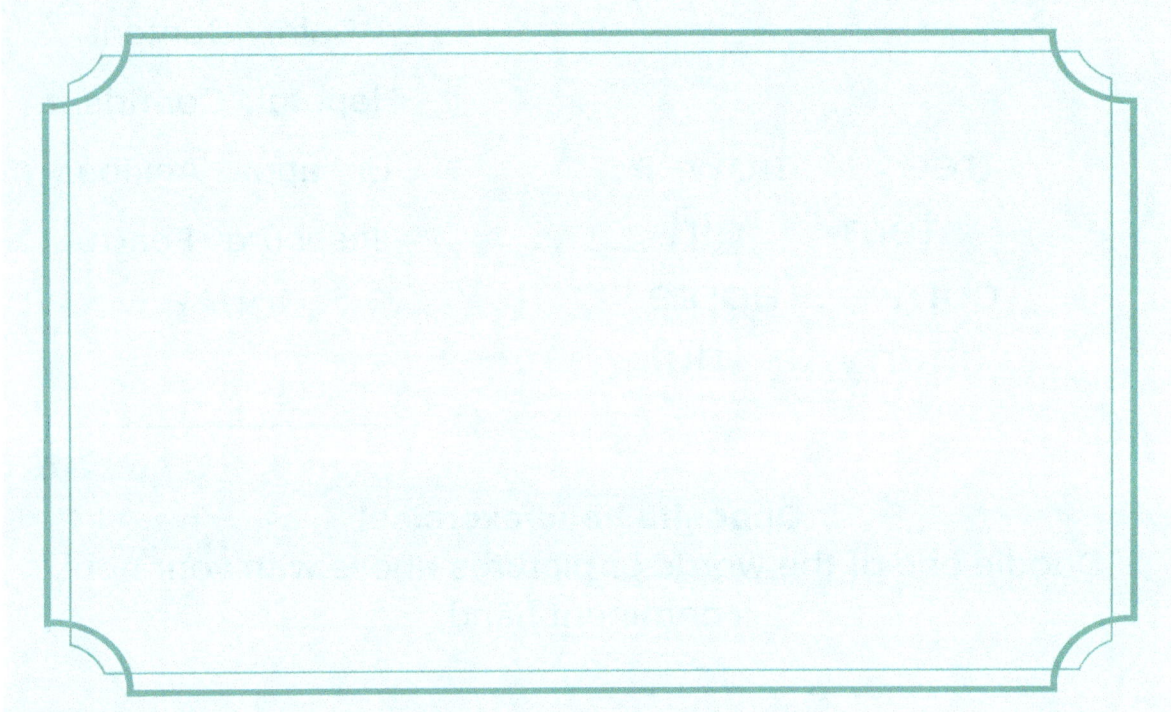

New Word for YOU

community
a group of neighbours who live close together
or people who have shared interests - artists community
Use it in a sentence:

_____

_____

_____

Memory Booster

Study the words or images for **60 seconds**, then list as many as you can remember on the next page.

My Mood Today. Circle one.

Happy
Calm   Content
Hopeful   Confident
Unhappy   Anxious
Insecure   Fearful
Other

_____

Opposite hand exercise!
Doodle one of the words or pictures above with your non-dominant hand.

Sleep Quality Last Night:

Super!   Good   Restless   Poor

Memory Booster

List as many words as you can remember
from the previous page... no peeking!

New Word for YOU

democracy
A form of government where the power rests with the people,
often through their through elected representatives
Use it in a sentence:

_____

_____

_____

Memory Booster

Study the words or images for **60 seconds**, then list as many as you can remember on the next page.

My Mood Today. Circle one.

Happy

Calm   Content

Hopeful   Confident

Unhappy   Anxious

Insecure   Fearful

Other

_____

Opposite hand exercise!
Doodle one of the words or pictures above with your non-dominant hand.

Sleep Quality Last Night:

Super!   Good   Restless   Poor

Memory Booster

List as many words as you can remember from the previous page... no peeking!

New Word for YOU

leisure
free time from work or something which takes up your time.
'at your liesure' - when you have time.
Use it in a sentence:

_____

_____

_____

Memory Booster

Study the words or images for **60 seconds**, then list as many as you can remember on the next page.

running

tongue

dachshund   strawberry

My Mood Today.
Circle one.

Happy

Calm   Content

Hopeful   Confident

Unhappy   Anxious

Insecure   Fearful

Other

_____

Opposite hand exercise!
Doodle one of the words or pictures above with your non-dominant hand.

Sleep Quality Last Night:

Super!   Good   Restless   Poor

Memory Booster

List as many words as you can remember
from the previous page... no peeking!

New Word for YOU

delicate
a thing of beauty; something or someone that is fragile
fine or liable to break; a light touch
Use it in a sentence:

_____

_____

_____

Memory Booster

Study the words or images for **60 seconds**, then list as many as you can remember on the next page.

My Mood Today. Circle one.

Happy

Calm   Content

Hopeful   Confident

Unhappy   Anxious

Insecure   Fearful

Other

_____

Opposite hand exercise!
Doodle one of the words or pictures above with your non-dominant hand.

Sleep Quality Last Night:

Super!   Good   Restless   Poor

Memory Booster

List as many words as you can remember from the previous page... no peeking!

New Word for YOU

hard yards
to have to put in a lot of hard work;
a real effort to get something done

Use it in a sentence:

_____

_____

_____

Memory Booster

Study the words or images for **60 seconds**, then list as many as you can remember on the next page.

My Mood Today. Circle one.

Happy
Calm   Content
Hopeful   Confident
Unhappy   Anxious
Insecure   Fearful
Other

_____

Opposite hand exercise!
Doodle one of the words or pictures above with your non-dominant hand.

Sleep Quality Last Night:

Super!   Good   Restless   Poor

Memory Booster

List as many words as you can remember from the previous page... no peeking!

New Word for YOU

repel
to drive someone or something back; to resist to feel disgust or sickened

Use it in a sentence:

_____

_____

_____

Memory Booster

Study the words or images for **60 seconds**, then list as many as you can remember on the next page.

scientist

table

leaves

rainbow

My Mood Today. Circle one.

Happy

Calm   Content

Hopeful   Confident

Unhappy   Anxious

Insecure   Fearful

Other

_____

Opposite hand exercise!
Doodle one of the words or pictures above with your non-dominant hand.

Sleep Quality Last Night:

Super!   Good   Restless   Poor

Memory Booster

List as many words as you can remember
from the previous page... no peeking!

New Word for YOU

temporary
something that is not permanent and lasts only a short time

Use it in a sentence:

_____

_____

_____

HOW DID YOU FEEL ABOUT THE GAMES YOU PLAYED?
CIRCLE ANY THAT APPLY.
YOU CAN EVEN ADD YOUR OWN!

GROUP GAME   GAME FOR 2

IT WAS SO FUNNY   I LIKE QUIET WORK   IT WAS OKAY

I LOVED IT   ?   MEH...

THIS WAS FUN   IT WAS CONFUSING

AHEM... NAILED IT!   NEW TO ME

Thank you
for buying this book!
Please write a few words as a review

Please check my website
www.kayenutman-writer.com
or Amazon for more books in the **Sudoku Puzzles** range, and other books by me. If you'd like printable versions, you'll find them on my website and on Etsy.com too.
You can join my author group on Facebook at
Kaye Nutman – Author
www.facebook.com/groups/360878484067782
where you'll se lots of interesting things and learn about other things I produce as a hybrid writer.

Kaye Nutman

oggytheoggdesign

★ Now turn the page for your free bookmark ★

Bonus
Make Your Own Bookmarks

Things you can do to make these useful bookmarks even better!

- Colour the second bookmark in your favourite colours.
- You can flip the second bookmark over and stick it to the back of the first bookmark

OR

- Stick the bookmarks onto card (you won't need to do this if you have a laminator).
- Allow a few mm border around each bookmark as you cut it out.
- If you have use of a laminating machine, put the bookmarks between the clear film with a space in between or just the one double sided bookmark.
- After lamination, cut out the shapes leaving a few mm border.
- Punch a hole in the top where the circle is.
- Add something – a tassel, a few beads on some wire, a small charm, etc.

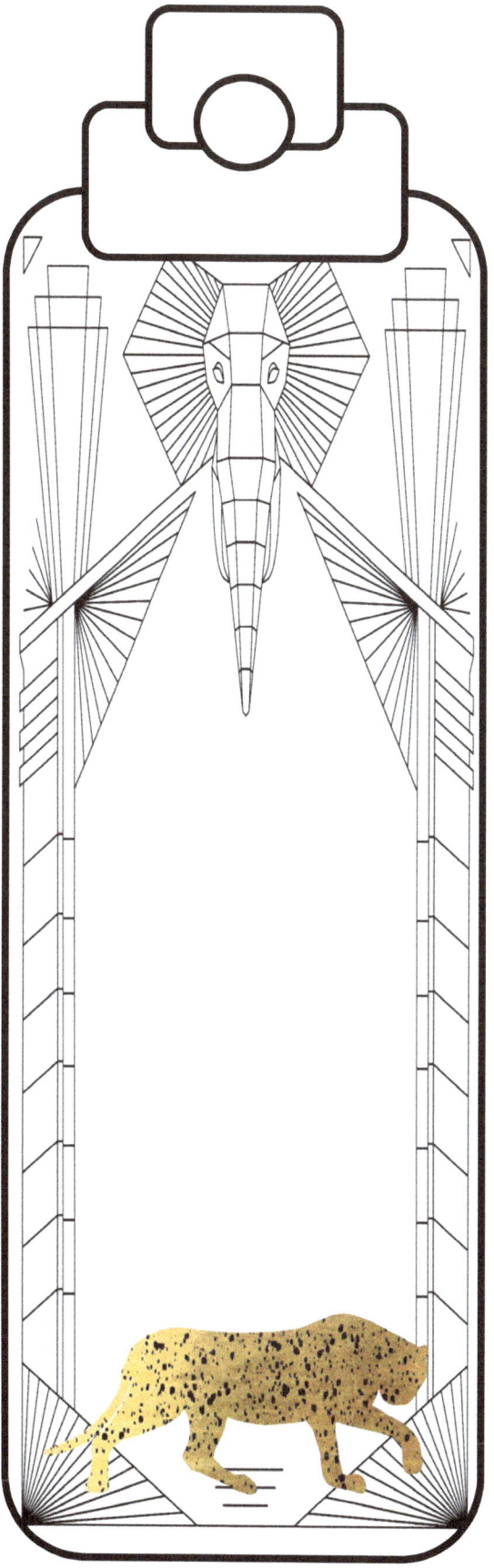

www.ingramcontent.com/pod-product-compliance
Lightning Source LLC
Chambersburg PA
CBHW060522010526
44107CB00060B/2654